SURPRISING SCIENCE

Fireworks

Dana Meachen Rau

mc Marshall Cavendish
Benchmark
New York

For the teachers of Lake Garda School, who make a big impact
—D.M.R.

Other Marshall Cavendish Offices:
Marshall Cavendish International (Asia) Private Limited, 1 New Industrial Road, Singapore 536196 • Marshall Cavendish International (Thailand) Co Ltd. 253 Asoke, 12th Flr, Sukhumvit 21 Road, Klongtoey Nua, Wattana, Bangkok 10110, Thailand • Marshall Cavendish (Malaysia) Sdn Bhd, Times Subang, Lot 46, Subang Hi-Tech Industrial Park, Batu Tiga, 40000 Shah Alam, Selangor Darul Ehsan, Malaysia

Marshall Cavendish is a trademark of Times Publishing Limited.

All websites were available and accurate when this book was sent to press.

Editor: Christina Gardeski
Publisher: Michelle Bisson
Art Director: Anahid Hamparian
Series Designer: Virginia Pope

Printed in Malaysia (T)
1 3 5 6 4 2

Library of Congress Cataloging-in-Publication Data
Rau, Dana Meachen, 1971–
Fireworks / by Dana Meachen Rau.
p. cm. — (Bookworms chapter books. Surprising science)
Summary: "Discusses the basic scientific principles and historical context of fireworks" —Provided by publisher.
Includes bibliographical references and index.
ISBN 978-0-7614-4868-6
1. Fireworks—Juvenile literature. I. Title.
TP300.R38 2011
662'.1--dc22
2009053723

Photo research by Connie Gardner

Cover photo by John Gillmoure/Corbis

The photographs in this book are used by permission and through the courtesy of: *Corbis*: pp. 4(L), 8(L), 12(L), 16(L) John Gillmoure; p. 4(R) Matthew Cavanaugh; p. 11(T) Bettmann; p. 14(L) Benelux; p. 15 Tobias Schwarz. *SuperStock*: p. 8(R); p. 10 Image Asset Management. *Getty Images*: pp. 1, 19 Pete Turner; p. 7 Steve Kelley; p. 20 Scott Berbour; p. 21 Michael Venera. *AP Photo*: p. 5 Anai Givon; p. 6 Matt Slocum; p. 12(R) Rick Rycroft; p. 14(R) JD Pooley; p. 18 Amendolara-Koester. *The Granger Collection*: pp. 9, 11(B). *PhotoEdit*: p. 13 Kayte Deloma. *The Image Works*: p. 16(R) H.G. Ross/Classic Stock; p. 17 Tiffany M. Hermon.

Fireworks

CHAPTER 1

Fireworks light up the night sky at a Washington, D.C., celebration.

Oooh! Aaah!

Fireworks explode over the city of Hong Kong for Chinese New Year.

Have you ever sat outside in the grass or on a picnic blanket waiting for fireworks to start? They begin slowly. One bang, then another. They get faster. You hear a whistle, then see a shower of light. The dark night becomes bright. More fireworks rise from the ground. They explode high above your head. They burst. They boom. They **bloom**. A fireworks show is an amazing sight.

Baseball games often end with the burst and bang of fireworks.

On the Fourth of July, many towns in the United States shoot off fireworks at parties and picnics. The Chinese welcome the New Year with loud firecrackers and bursts of light. Fans at a baseball game may cheer at a display on a summer night. People like to celebrate with fireworks.

People watch fireworks from buildings and boats on the Fourth of July.

7

CHAPTER 2

Fireworks often marked special occasions for English royalty.

Fireworks History

About one thousand years ago, the Chinese mixed different **chemicals** to make medicines. They discovered that one mixture flamed, smoked, and made a loud sound when lit with fire. This mixture came to be known as gunpowder. Soldiers used it to make flaming arrows, fireballs, and later to shoot bullets from guns. The Chinese also made rockets with gunpowder. These rockets shot into the sky, then exploded with showers of sparks. They **launched** these early fireworks at weddings, holidays, and other parties. They believed the loud noise scared away evil spirits.

Explorers and soldiers from Europe visited China

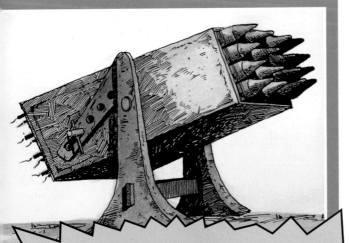

Ancient Chinese firework-makers used the power of gunpowder to launch fireworks.

The craftsmen who made fireworks had an important job—to entertain crowds with impressive displays.

in the 1200s. They saw fireworks for the first time and brought some home with them. The Italians opened many fireworks factories. For the next few hundred years, they made fireworks for all sorts of celebrations. Kings and queens used them to celebrate the birth of a new prince or princess. People set up pretend battles and launched fireworks from boats. They also made buildings from wood and cloth called **temples**. The temples were decorated with fountains of light, statues lit up with fireworks, and spinning wheels spraying fiery sparks.

Parades included fireworks, too. In England in the 1600s and 1700s, a "green man" led the parade. His job was to clear the way. He swung a fire club that shot off sparks. He wore a hat of leaves to protect his head.

People often set off fireworks from boats in the harbor.

Some of the early colonists in America held displays. On July 4, 1776, America said it was a separate country from Britain. Beginning in 1777, and ever since, Independence Day on the Fourth of July has been celebrated with fireworks.

At first, fireworks just came in yellow and orange. People tried different chemicals to make new colors. By the 1800s, they knew how to make red and green. In the 1900s, they added blue and purple. Today, fireworks come in all colors.

In 1886, New Yorkers celebrated their new Statue of Liberty with fireworks.

CHAPTER 3

An expert prepares fireworks for a New Year's celebration in Sydney, Australia.

How Fireworks Work

Fireworks are possible because of a science called **chemistry**. Chemistry is the study of how certain chemicals act when they are mixed, heated, or changed. A firework uses fire to burn the chemicals.

Firecrackers and sparklers are simple fireworks. A firecracker is made of powdered chemicals wrapped in a strong paper tube. It has a **fuse** coming out one end. The fuse is like the wick of a candle. When the fuse is lit, it burns down until it reaches the powder. The powder

Colorful fireworks come in colorful packages.

13

Above: A firecracker has a fuse that burns down to the powder. The powder is wrapped in a paper tube. Right: A sparkler is a firework on a stick!

is the **fuel** for the firecracker. When the powder burns, its chemicals make **gases**. These gases build up pressure inside the firecracker. They push outward until the firecracker explodes. The sudden "crack" of the firecracker is the sound of the paper tube tearing apart.

A sparkler is a metal wire dipped in chemicals. When the sparkler is lit, the chemicals burn. Little bits of metal mixed with the chemicals glow and make lots of sparks.

A firework that shoots up into the sky is called an **aerial shell**. It is held together by tightly wound paper. To launch the shell, a person

An aerial shell is placed in a long tube that will launch it into the sky.

places it into the bottom of a **mortar**. A mortar is a long tube sticking up from the ground. The fuse is lit. The fuse reaches a pocket of powder called the lift charge in the bottom of the mortar. The lift charge burns and explodes. This launches the shell high into the air. Liftoff!

The rest of the firework doesn't burn right away. The fuse is long. The shell goes to its highest point in the sky. Then the flame on the fuse reaches the next pocket of powder in the center of the shell called the burst charge. When this powder explodes, the shell bursts open.

The explosion lights chemicals that make dots of color. It sprays them into the sky.

CHAPTER 4

You can see why the dots of light that fall from the sky from fireworks are called "stars"!

Amazing Displays

There are many types of fireworks. Some burst like blooming flowers or waterfalls. Some have one color. Others have many. Some burst more than once in the sky. Some are arranged on a frame to create a picture. Some make a loud bang!

The parts of a firework that create the dots of color are called **stars**. These stars are made of chemicals and metals.

Some fireworks look like blooming flowers.

Different chemicals and metals make different colors.

Some fireworks make different shapes because of the way the stars are packed into the shell. If the stars are scattered around the center, the explosion will make a flower shape. If they are arranged in a circle, the firework makes a ring. Stars can be set up to make the shape of hearts, flags, or even smiley faces.

In many states, it is against the law to set off fireworks at home. This is because people can be hurt or killed by them. Even when it isn't against the law, only adults should set off fireworks. Fireworks should never be used indoors or in a closed container. They should never be set off near people or anything that can

In this oversized model of a firework, you can see how the parts are arranged to make a star shape.

Fireworks fill the dark evening with sparkling bursts of light and booming blasts of sound.

catch fire. A bucket of water, garden hose, or fire extinguisher should be kept nearby, just in case.

Setting off fireworks is best left to experts at public displays. Before big events, they spend a long time setting up the mortars and shells. They make sure the site is safe. They set up a **control panel** so they can launch fireworks without having to light the fuse by hand.

Fireworks can be seen
from many miles.

Some fireworks displays are controlled by computers. Shows are often set to music. The shells go off to match the tune. The loudest and biggest fireworks explode for a big ending!

For a thousand years, people have enjoyed watching amazing displays of shapes and colors in the sky. We still use fireworks for the same reason. To celebrate!

Happy Independence Day! Celebrate with fireworks.

Glossary

aerial shell [AIR-ee-uhl SHEL] a firework filled with powdered chemicals wrapped in a paper cover that is shot into the air

bloom [BLOOM] to make a pattern with lines coming out from a center point, like a flower

chemicals [KEM-i-kuhls] substances found in the earth or created by mixing, heating, or changing them

chemistry [KEM-uh-stree] the study of how certain substances act when they are mixed, heated, or changed

control panel [kuhn-TROHL PAN-l] a device that can do a job from a safe distance

fuel [FYOO-uhl] something that creates energy when burned

fuse [FYOOZ] a cord that burns slowly

gases [GAS-es] substances in the air

launched [LAWNCHT] to shoot up very fast

mortar [MAWR-ter] a long tube that sticks up from the ground and holds a firework

stars [STAHRS] the parts of a firework that create the dots of color

temples [TEM-puhls] a structure made from wood and cloth used to display fireworks

Books to Discover

Cobb, Vicki. *Where's the Science Here? Fireworks*. Minneapolis, MN: Millbrook Press, 2006.

Dotz, Warren. *Firecrackers: The Art and History*. Berkeley, CA: Ten Speed Press, 2004.

Otto, Carolyn. *Celebrate Chinese New Year: With Fireworks, Dragons, and Lanterns*. Washington, DC: National Geographic Children's Books, 2009.

Parker, Steve. *Chemicals and Change*. Langhorne, PA: Chelsea House Publishers, 2005.

Thomas, Isabel. *Fireworks! Chemical Reactions*. Chicago, IL: Heinemann-Raintree, 2007.

Websites to Explore

The Art and Science of Fireworks Displays
http://geology.com/articles/fireworks/

How Fireworks Work
www.howstuffworks.com/fireworks.htm

The National Council on Fireworks Safety www.fireworksafety.com/

Nova Online: Fireworks www.pbs.org/wgbh/nova/fireworks/

Index

About the Author

Dana Meachen Rau is the author of more than 250 books for children. She has written about many nonfiction topics from her home office in Burlington, Connecticut. When Mrs. Rau was young, she used to hide inside during the fireworks at the annual Fourth of July picnic. Today, she enjoys the thrill of a bright, colorful fireworks finale.

With thanks to the Reading Consultants:

Nanci R. Vargus, Ed.D., is an assistant professor of elementary education at the University of Indianapolis.

Beth Walker Gambro is an adjunct professor at the University of Saint Francis in Joliet, Illinois.